Thanks

Marcia & David Kapla

The material in this book has been compiled over a long period of time. Many of the sources are unknown to the compilers. We wish to acknowledge the original authors whoever they may be.

ISBN: 0-9617744-4-4

*This book is dedicated
to those we think of,
those we care for,
those we love.*

Hearts, like doors,
Will open with ease
to very, very little keys,
And don't forget
that two of these
are "I thank you"
and "If you please."

We are never so charitable as when there is no one but ourselves to blame.

If you haven't much to be thankful for, be thankful for what you don't have.

*Each day is a gift.
Receive it with
thankfulness, Unwrap
it with anticipation,
and relish it with joy!*

Life is like a ten-speed bike. Most of us have gears we never use.

— Charles M. Schulz

If you have a clear conscience
and good health,
If you have a few good friends
and a happy home,
If your heart has kept its youth
and your soul it's honesty,
then cheer up — you are still
one of life's fortunate millionaires.

Appreciation is like an insurance policy. You have to keep renewing it.

If you think practice makes perfect, you have never tried to raise kids.

May you have warm words
on a cold evening,
A full moon
on a dark night,
And the road downhill
all the way to your door.

Kindness is like snow;
it makes everything it
covers beautiful.

Friends are family you choose for yourself.

Some people know the way
to make each day seem more worthwhile,
They do the nicest things
for you and always wear a smile,
They make this world a better place
by practicing the art
of reaching out to others
and by giving from the heart.

...Amanda Bradley

Reach down and lift others up. It's the best exercise you can get.

*Set a shining
example today
and tomorrow
will be much
brighter.*

The most powerful single thing you can do to have influence over others is to smile at them.

The greatest ability is dependability.

Curt Bergwall

Pray for a good harvest, but continue to hoe, hoe, hoe!

*I like chocolate
ice cream — but,
when I go
fishing, I use
worms, 'cause
fish like worms.*

If a man leaves children behind him, it is as if he did not die.

Moroccan Proverb

Praise does wonders for our sense of hearing.

— *Arnold Glasgow*

It is not always easy to…

Apologize
begin over
take advice
be unselfish
keep on trying
be considerate
think and then act
profit by mistakes
forgive and forget
shoulder the blame
…but it usually pays.

If you are feeling low,
don't despair.
The sun has a sinking spell
every night,
but comes back up
every morning.

*Sitting still and wishing
makes no person great.
The good Lord sends the fishing,
But you must dig the bait.*

Success is doing the things other people say they're going to do.

Ideas are a dime a dozen — and the men and women who implement them are priceless.

The trouble with learning from experience is that you never graduate.

Doug Larson

*There is no
modern pain
medicine as
effective as a
mother's kiss.*

Never look down on a person unless you are helping him up.

Optimism is a cheerful frame of mind that enables a tea kettle to sing though in hot water up to its neck.

Success comes in cans.
Failure comes in can'ts.

One person with a belief is equal to 99 with only interest.

*It's never too
late to be what
you might have
been.*

George Eliott

What wisdom can you find that is greater than kindness.

...Jean-Jacques Rousseau

KNOCK KNOCK!

When opportunity knocks, make sure you're not in the backyard looking for four leaf clovers.

It is often surprising to find out what heights may be attained merely by remaining on the level.

An optimist goes to the window every morning and says, "Good morning, God."

The pessimist goes to the window and says, "Good God, it's morning!"

May you always find three welcomes -

In a garden during summer.
At a fireside during winter.
And whatever the season
In the kind eyes of a friend.

If you are willing to admit you are wrong when you are wrong, you're all right.

Our business in life is not to see through one another, it is to see one another through.

...Peter DeVries

A smile is worth a million but it doesn't cost a cent.

Henry C. Mabry

*It is better to
know some of the
questions, than
all
of the
answers.*

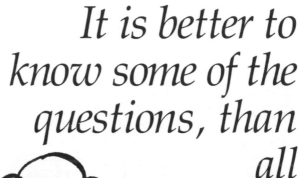

James Thurber

One good thing about punctuality is that it's a sure way to help you enjoy a few minutes of privacy.

Money will buy a fine dog, but only kindness will make it wag its tail.

*If someone asks,
"When is my ship
going to come in?"
Remind them
that steam
has replaced
wind.*

One of the best things people can have up their sleeves is a funny bone.

...Richard L. Weaver II

Love is a priceless commodity. It is the only thing you can give away and still keep.

There is plenty of room at the top, but no room to sit down.

*The very best
way to get
credit is to try
to give it away.*

*The best things you
can give children,
next to good habits,
are good memories.*

...*Sydney J. Harris*

It is one of the most beautiful compensations of life that no man can sincerely try to help another without helping himself.

...Emerson

The glory of springtime is the same to all. But, there are many different points of view. A child sees it best from the middle of a mud puddle.

*As much of heaven
is visible as we
have eyes to see.*

…William Winter

MacGregor's Law:

The first one to see a traffic light turn green is the second car back.

A hug is the perfect gift — one size fits all, and nobody minds if you exchange it.

Ivern Ball

*No one stands
as straight as
when he stoops
to help
someone.*

*A well-adjusted parent
is one who can enjoy
the scenery even
with the kids in the
back seat.*

The way I see it, if you want the rainbow, you gotta put up with the rain.

...Dolly Parton

One of the most difficult things to give away is kindness — it is usually returned.

...Cort R. Flint

*There is always
sunshine, only we
must do our part;
we must move
into it.*

...C.L. Burnham

Sometimes the smallest things in life are the hardest to take. You can sit on a mountain more comfortably than on a tack. OUCH!

*If you want
people to swallow
what you say,
always use lots of
shortening.*

*Blessed are the flexible,
for they shall not be
bent out of shape.*

…Michael McGriff, M.D.

He who receives a good turn should never forget it;
He who does a good turn should never remember it.

...Charron

Life is 10 % what you make it. And 90 % how you take it.

Irving Berlin

Cheerfulness is the window cleaner of the mind.

There is music in all hearts. If we listen, we can hear each other's song.

It is the lifted face that feels the shining of the sun.

...Browning

Anytime you think you have influence, try ordering around someone else's dog.

The Cockle Bar

Anyone who isn't pulling his weight is probably pushing his luck.

The world doesn't want to hear about the labor pains, they just want to see the baby.

A good neighbor doubles the value of a house.

...*German Proverb*

What kills a skunk is the publicity it gives itself.

Abraham Lincoln

Life… it's like a piano. What you get out of it depends on how you play it.

Thanksgiving comes but once a year, but reasons to give thanks are always here.

A smile is an inexpensive way to improve your looks.

Why is it that the wettest dogs are always the friendliest dogs?

There are two ways to get to the top of an oak tree — Sit on an acorn and wait or climb it!

*Everytime a child
is born the world
lights up with new
possibilities.*

The pleasure of life is according to the man that lives it, and not according to the work or place.

Emerson

Success seems largely to be a matter of hanging on after others have let go.

...William Feather

Make the most of the best and the least of the worst.

...*Robert Louis Stevenson*

*Be glad of life
because it gives
you the chance
to love and
to work and
to play and
to look up
at the
stars.*

Henry Van Dyke

A happy person is not a person in a certain set of circumstances, but rather a person with a certain set of attitudes.

...Hugh Downs

The man who makes no mistakes does not usually make anything.

Bishop Magee

One good turn usually gets the whole blanket.

A single reason why you can do something is worth a hundred reasons why you can't.

*Life is like golf —
Forget the score and
keep on swinging.*

*Making a wish
that you'll always
enjoy life…
always have good
health and good
friends… and find
a harvest of happy
memories each
year.*

USE THIS CONVENIENT ORDER FORM FOR ADDITIONAL
COPIES OF ALL THE KAPLAN BOOKS

NAME _____

ADDRESS _____

CITY _____

STATE _____ ZIP CODE _____

I WOULD LIKE TO ORDER:

     CHEERS BOOKS @ $5.95

     SMILES BOOKS @ $5.95

     FRIENDS BOOKS @ $5.95

     HAPPINESS BOOKS @ $5.95

     THANKS BOOKS @ $5.95

     3 BOOK SETS WITH SLIP COVER @ $17.50
     (CHEERS, SMILES, FRIENDS)

PLEASE SEND ORDER FORM AND CHECK OR MONEY ORDER
TO: **CHEERS, P.O. BOX 550513, ATLANTA, GA. 30355-3013**

USE THIS CONVENIENT ORDER FORM FOR ADDITIONAL
COPIES OF ALL THE KAPLAN BOOKS

NAME _____

ADDRESS _____

CITY _____

STATE _____ ZIP CODE _____

I WOULD LIKE TO ORDER:

     CHEERS BOOKS @ $5.95

     SMILES BOOKS @ $5.95

     FRIENDS BOOKS @ $5.95

     HAPPINESS BOOKS @ $5.95

     THANKS BOOKS @ $5.95

     3 BOOK SETS WITH SLIP COVER @ $17.50
     (CHEERS, SMILES, FRIENDS)

PLEASE SEND ORDER FORM AND CHECK OR MONEY ORDER
TO: **CHEERS, P.O. BOX 550513, ATLANTA, GA. 30355-3013**